Handwriting Practice Bible

Children's Reading & Writing Education Books

BABY PROFESSOR
EDUCATION KIDS

Speedy Publishing LLC
40 E. Main St. #1156
Newark, DE 19711
www.speedypublishing.com

Practice Writing

Trace and rewrite the following bible verses.

If God be for us, who can be against us?

—Romans 8:31

If you can believe, all things are possible to him who believes.

— Mark 9:23

Whatever you do, do it heartily, as to the Lord and not to men.

— Colossians 3:23

I can do everything through
him who gives me strength.
— Phil 4:13

Your word is a lamp to my feet and a light to my path.

— Psalm 119:105

Rejoice in the Lord always.

Again I say, rejoice

— Philippians 4:4

In the day of my trouble I will call on You, for You will answer me.

— Psalm 86:7

Dont let your hearts be

troubled. Trust in God, and

trust also in me.

— John 1:41

I can do all things through

Christ who strengthens me.

– Philippians 4:13

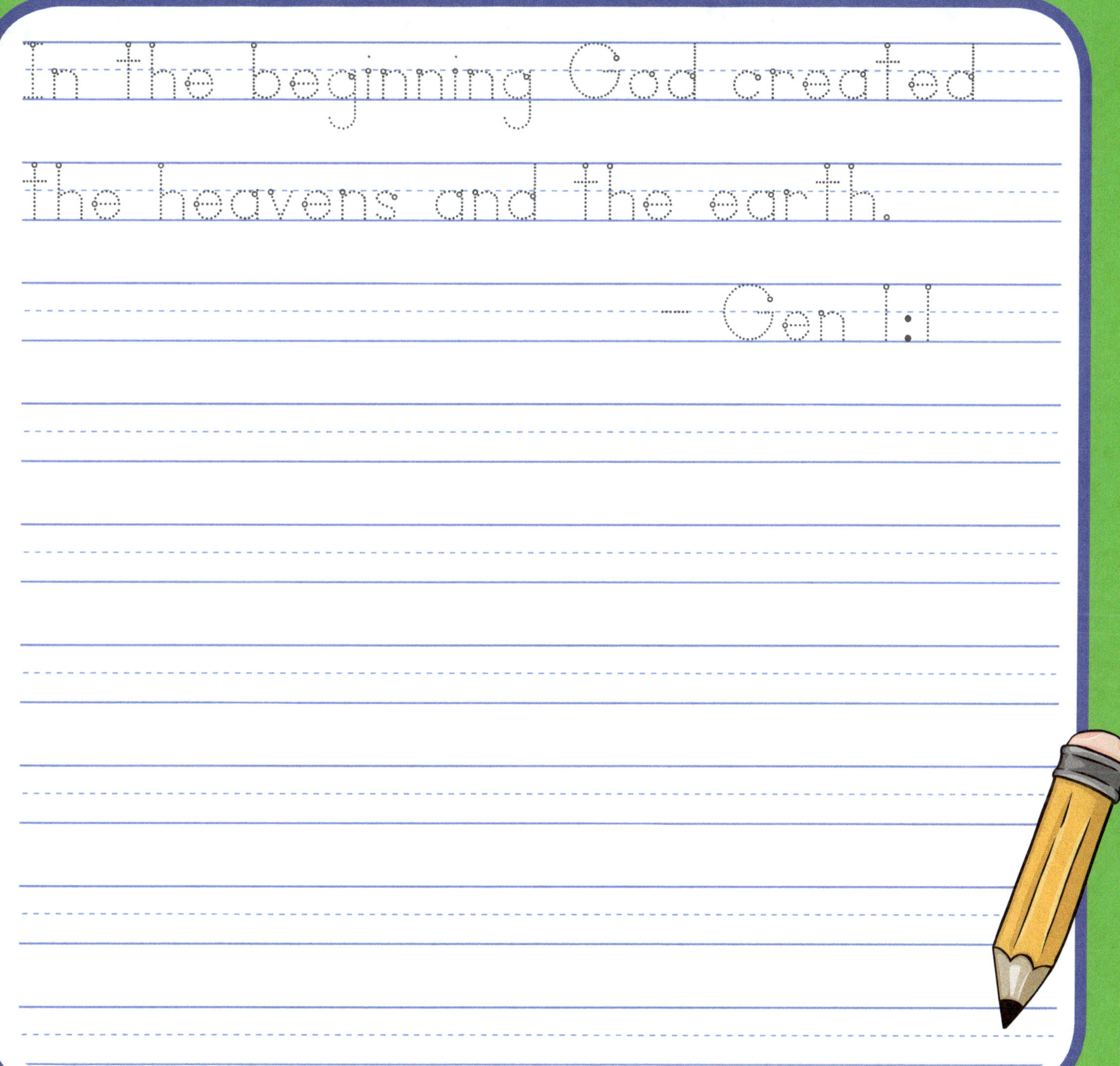
In the beginning God created
the heavens and the earth.
– Gen 1:1

Yet in all these things, we are more than conquerors through Him who loved us.

—Rom 8:37

We know that we live in him and he in us, because he has given us of his Spirit.

— I John 4:13 NIV

So encourage each other and build each other up, just as you are already doing.

— 1 Thessalonians 5:11

Come to me, all you who are weary and burdened, and I will give you rest.

— Matt 11:28

But the fruit of the Spirit is
love, joy, peace, patience,
kindness, goodness, faithfulness,
— Gal 5:22

gentleness and self-control.

Against such things there is no

law.

— Gal 5:23

Now faith is being sure of
what we hope for and certain
of what we do not see.

—Heb 11:1

How good and pleasant it is
when brothers live together in
unity

—Ps 133:1

Delight yourself in the LORD
and he will give you the desires
of your heart.

— Ps 37:4

Whatever you do, work at it
with all your heart, as working
for the Lord, not for men

— Col 3:23

You will keep in perfect peace
him whose mind is steadfast,
because he trusts in you.

– Isa 26:3

Greater love has no one than this, that he lay down his life for his friends.

– John 15:13

because you know that the

testing of your faith develops

perseverance.

— Jas 1:3

For my yoke is easy and my burden is light.

— Matt 11:30

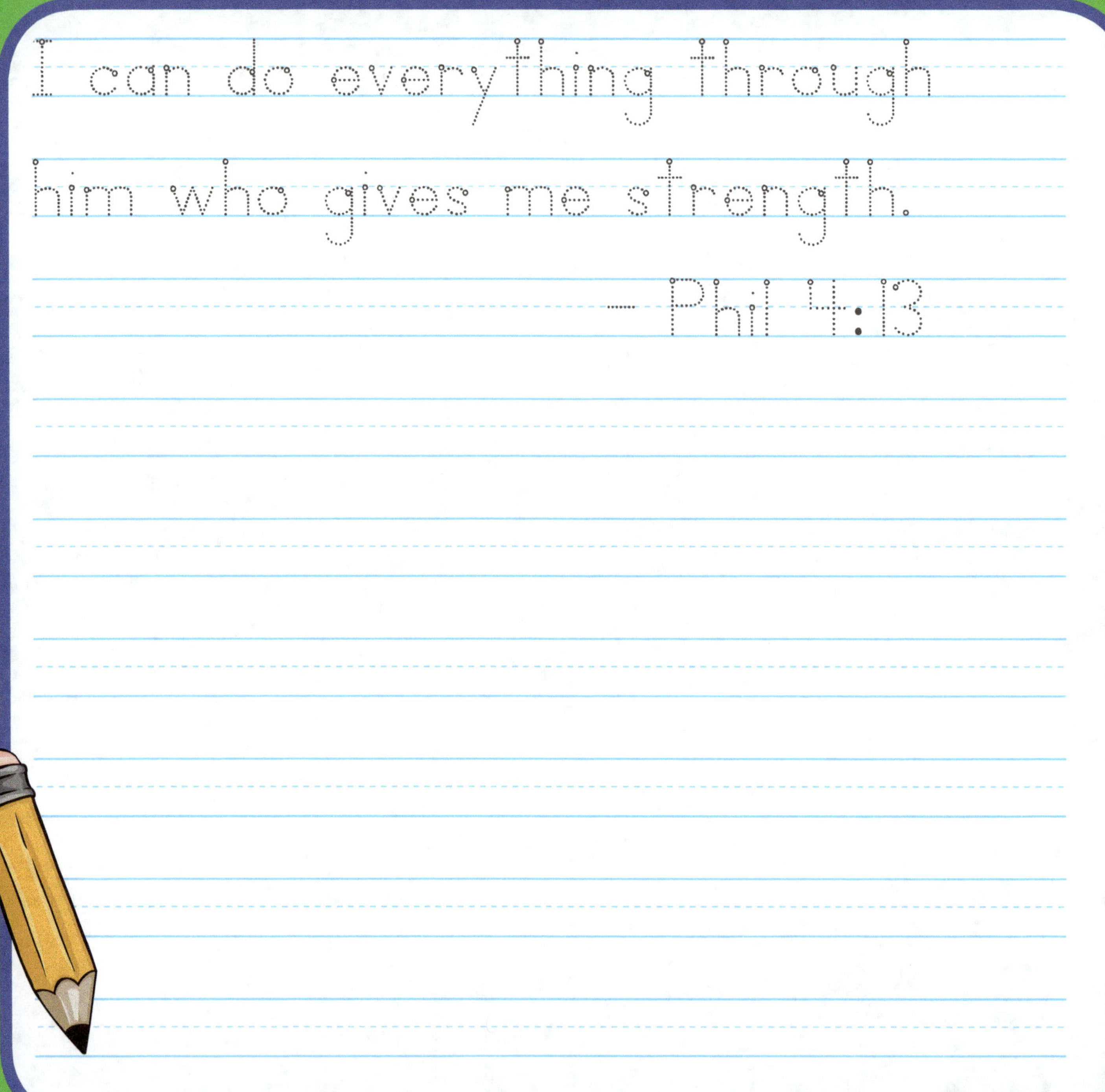
I can do everything through
him who gives me strength.
— Phil 4:13

Believe on the Lord Jesus
Christ, and you will be saved.

—Act 16:31

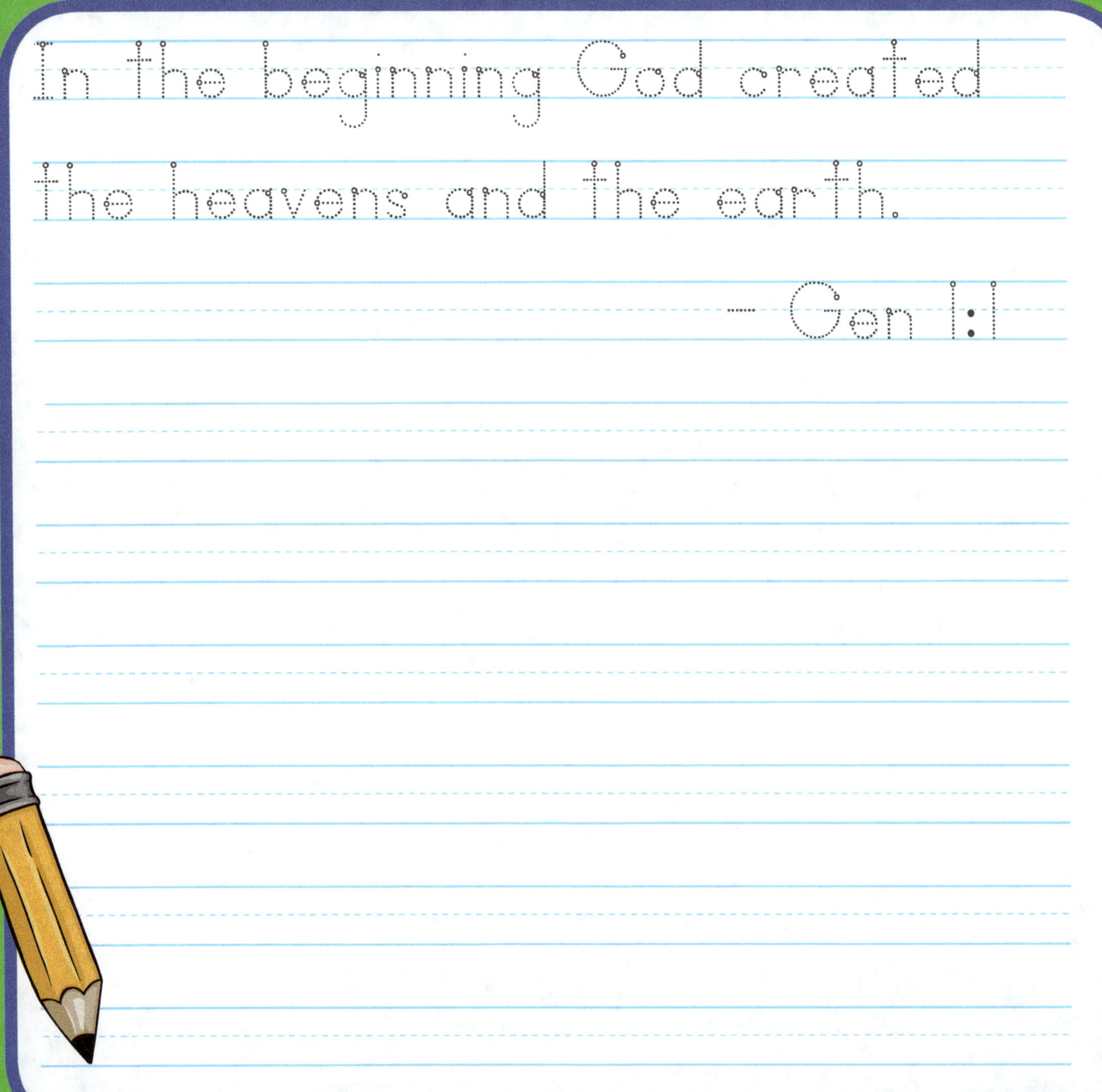

In the beginning God created
the heavens and the earth.
— Gen 1:1

for all have sinned and fall

short of the glory of God,

– Rom 3:23

Set your minds on things above,
not on earthly things.

— Col 3:2

Let the word of Christ dwell

in you richly

— Col 3:16

This is love for God to obey his commands

—1 John 5:3

And do not grieve the Holy Spirit

– Eph 4:30

Jesus Christ is the same

yesterday, today and forever.

— Heb:13 8

Let everything that has breath praise the Lord.

—Psalm 150:6

Trust in the Lord with all your heart.

– Prov 3:5

Everyone who calls on the
name of the Lord will be saved.
— Rom 10:13

www.ingramcontent.com/pod-product-compliance
Lightning Source LLC
LaVergne TN
LVHW080357180826
845678LV00025B/1964

* 9 7 9 8 8 6 9 4 4 8 9 0 3 *